salad dressings

By Jessica Strand

Photographs by Maren Caruso

CHRONICLE BOOKS

SAN FRANCISCO

ISBN 10: 08118-5238-5
ISBN 13: 978-08118-5238-8

Manufactured in China.

Design and typesetting by Carole Goodman /
    Blue Anchor Design
Food and prop styling: EK Food Productions
Photographer's assistants: Faiza Ali and Christine Wells
Food stylist's assistants: Naomi Crawford and
    Mark Harris

10 9 8 7 6 5 4 3 2 1

Chronicle Books LLC
85 Second Street
San Francisco, California 94105

www.chroniclebooks.com

Tabasco is a registered trademark of McIlhenny Co.

DEDICATION

To Tracy and Les—my salad-eating friends.

ACKNOWLEDGMENTS

I have so many wonderful people to thank for helping me to put this book together so quickly and so beautifully. Without the tireless, energetic staff at Chronicle Books where would I be? Thank you, Maren Caruso, Carole Goodman, Laurel Leigh, Pamela Geismar, Kevin Toyama, and Catherine Huchting. I must offer a special thanks to my talented editor Leslie Jonath, who makes every project a joy. I also thank my husband, Stephen, and my dear friend Tracy, who spent hours with me in the kitchen as we tested and tasted innumerable salads and salad dressings. There was another set of small hands in the kitchen stirring and blending: my son, Lucian, who is every mother's dream sous-chef. Thank you, Bunny, for being you.

TABLE OF CONTENTS

INTRODUCTION

WHEN I THINK OF A SALAD, THE FIRST THING THAT COMES TO MIND IS A large wooden bowl filled with freshly washed greens. On top of the greens are slices of pale green avocado, thinly sliced red onion, glistening slivers of red pepper, and lots of odd-shaped, tiny yellow, bright red, and deep orange tomatoes. I dress the salad in a vinaigrette of Dijon mustard, garlic, lemon, good balsamic vinegar, salt, freshly ground black pepper, and lots of cloudy, deep green extra-virgin olive oil. When dressed, the greens become more complex, the avocado seems creamier, the red pepper appears crisper, and the tomatoes taste even sweeter.

Salads come in endless varieties! There are the starchy ones made with noodles, rice, or potatoes. The seafood varieties are made with every fish and shellfish imaginable. And the most substantial of all, the meaty dishes include tender strips of steak, succulent morsels of chicken, or razor-thin slices of pork. The dressing adds the final touch to both light and hearty salads and defines their flavor.

Since the dressing plays such a key part in creating a divine salad, it's important to pair it correctly with the ingredients. If a dressing doesn't hold up to the components of the salad, the balance is thrown off; conversely when a dressing is too powerful, it's impossible to taste any of the fixings. When matching a dressing to the salad's ingredients, there are a few rules to follow:

1. Delicate, tender greens and raw, young vegetables go well with a light, herbal vinaigrette consisting of oil and vinegar or lemon. For additional flavor and a little more heft, add a sprinkling of a salty, crumbly cheese such as Greek or French feta, a goat cheese, or a mild blue cheese (Saga Blue, American blues).

2. Creamy dressings and thick vinaigrettes go well with fish, meat, or starchy salads, which include ingredients that can match the dressings with their own hearty flavor or texture.

3. Exotic dressings can be used like creamy mixtures and thick vinaigrettes to add a distinctive, unusual flavor to a variety of hearty ingredients.

The combination of salad ingredients and the choice of dressing are matched in importance by the quality of the ingredients used to create them. If you choose the freshest ingredients for your salad, and invest in some great staples for your dressing pantry, you can't go wrong in creating a mouth-watering salad. It's important to begin with a good, fruity virgin olive oil.

Consider a variety of interesting mustards, which will add an earthy depth. Of course, fresh and dried herbs also will help to create a more complex, flavorful dressing. Use only fresh garlic and ginger. If they aren't, they can give a decidedly bitter taste to a salad. Also make sure that your dried herbs have not been around for more than a year, since over time they lose their flavor. When it comes to a creamy dressing, think of the components separately and look for the smoothest, creamiest whole yogurt or sour cream. When buying cheese or miso, think about how rich or intense the flavors are. Creating a good salad is all about balance.

Dressing a salad is a tricky topic. My rule of thumb is dress it as much as you like. Whether a leaf is lightly brushed with dressing or completely saturated by it—it's all a matter of taste. When to dress a salad is a different matter. Some—including rice, potato, or chicken salads—benefit from marinating in the dressing, while the more delicate vegetables and greens become wilted and soggy if tossed prematurely. Most recipes will guide you through the process. Salads with crisp vegetables and greens shouldn't be dressed until right before they're served.

The longevity of a dressing depends on its ingredients. A plain vinaigrette can last as long as a month in the refrigerator until the taste begins to alter. If a vinaigrette has bacon, cheese, or egg in it, it won't last more than three to five days—the bacon will become too soggy, the cheese will lose its flavor, and the egg will decompose. Creamy dressings begin to separate and become watery within several days to a week. Opened or unopened vinegar lasts indefinitely, whereas after being opened, olive oil can last as long as three months on the shelf or as long as six to eight months in the refrigerator. If you refrigerate your olive oil, it hardens like any fat and needs to be taken out forty-five minutes to an hour before using so that it has time to warm to room temperature.

This book will guide you through the dressing-making process, with three categories of dressings including vinaigrettes, creamy mixtures, and more exotic recipes. Within each category you'll find simple, foolproof, and delicious recipes. I've also included salad recipes that will give you a better idea of how to pair various dressings and salad ingredients. The Salad Pantry list will help you to stock your pantry with all the essentials for future salad making. And, you'll find a handful of easy-to-make topping recipes like flavored nuts, croutons, and Parmesan crisps.

Grab that bowl and get ready to make a tasty, delicious dressing that will turn your ingredients into gold.

—Jessica Strand

SALAD PANTRY

Keep a variety of oils, vinegars, and specialty items on hand, and you'll always be able to adapt a salad recipe or invent your own.

Oils
Canola oil

Citrus-flavored olive oils

Extra-virgin olive oil

Sesame oil

Walnut oil

Vinegars
Balsamic vinegar

Champagne vinegar

Cider vinegar

Red wine vinegar

Rice wine vinegar

Spanish sherry vinegar

White wine vinegar

Sauces
Horseradish cream

Ponzu

Soy sauce

Worcestershire sauce

Mustards
Dijon mustard

Whole-grain mustard

Other Ingredients
Anchovies

Black peppercorns

Capers

Dried fruit: apricots, raisins, currants, cran-berries, blueberries, apples, prunes, and figs

Dried herbs: oregano, basil, dill, parsley, and thyme

Garlic

Honey

Lemons and limes

Nuts: almonds, walnuts, pecans, *pepitas* (pumpkin seeds), and sesame seeds

Olives: oil-cured black and Niçoise

Sea salt

Sugar

Sun-dried tomatoes

OILS AND VINEGARS

OLIVE OIL

It's difficult to translate the labels on the more than 150 brands of olive oil. Here's a quick guide to the various types of olive oil.

Estate bottled: These olives were grown and pressed at the same location.

Extra-virgin olive oil: This has the most intense flavor of the olive oils. It tastes green and nutty. It's considered the best quality because it is the smoothest and least acidic of all the olive oils.

Virgin olive oil: This has a higher acidity level than the extra-virgin variety, and though it is perfectly good on salads, it is less flavorful and a little more acidic.

Olive oil: This oil is less intense in color and flavor. It can be added to salad dressings but is better used for cooking.

OILS

Canola oil: It's my first choice for an alternative to olive oil. It's very mild in flavor and it goes with a variety of ingredients.

Toasted sesame oil: This Asian oil has a deep, nutty aroma and flavor. It is usually best when combined with another oil, such as canola.

Walnut oil: This wonderful, flavorful oil is terrific drizzled on most greens and followed by a splash of vinegar.

VINEGARS

Balsamic vinegar: This can be the priciest of vinegars depending on its quality. Though it's a deep brownish red color, it's made from white Trebbiano grapes and aged in wooden barrels. It has a deep, rich flavor and a syrupy texture. The best varieties come from Modena, Italy.

Champagne vinegar: Made from champagne grapes, this very delicate vinegar has a slightly sweet, slightly floral flavor. It's wonderful served with delicate greens, fruits, chicken, or fish.

Cider vinegar: This vinegar is as versatile as balsamic, with its apple flavor and acidic bite adding a nice tart edge to any dressing. Cider vinegar is made from apple cider.

Red or white wine vinegar: Wine vinegars are made with different types of red and white wines, and so the flavor depends upon the brand. White wine vinegars are very acidic and tangy and are not appropriate for all dressings, whereas red wine vinegars are a bit mellower in flavor since they are barrel aged.

Rice wine vinegar: This Asian vinegar is very mild in flavor. The Chinese version has a slightly bolder taste than the Japanese, which is very delicate. Japanese rice wine vinegar comes plain or seasoned.

Sherry vinegar: Try to buy a Spanish Sherry vinegar; they are by far the best and have a subtle, smooth flavor with a distinct tart finish. Sherry vinegar is versatile and can be used in most recipes where vinegar is listed.

Ponzu: Technically a sauce, this bottled Japanese sauce is a mixture of lemon juice, rice wine vinegar, and mirin, a sweet Japanese rice wine.

TOPPINGS

Toppings add that little extra crunch that makes a salad. I've included recipes for my favorites: flavored croutons, spiced nuts, and perfect, paper-thin Parmesan crisps.

Flavored Croutons

Homemade croutons are a wonderful addition to a salad. Think about the ingredients in your dressings and salad before you choose a flavor. It's best to use stale peasant bread for your croutons, but if you don't have any stale bread handy, just toast the bread for several minutes in the oven. You want to make sure it's beginning to dry out but not yet golden.

Basic Recipe

6 tablespoons virgin olive oil
6 thick slices of good, crusty peasant bread, cut into 1-inch cubes
1 teaspoon sea salt

In a medium cast-iron pan, place the oil over medium-low heat. When the oil begins to sizzle after 1 to 2 minutes, add the cubed bread. Turn the bread when it becomes golden and toast each side. Cover the bread with salt while it is still hot. Place on a paper towel to cool.

Makes 1½ cups

For Garlic Croutons: Add 5 to 6 garlic cloves to the oil. Let the garlic lightly brown on all sides for about 5 to 7 minutes. Discard the garlic or reserve it to add to your salad. The cloves lose their intensity when cooked whole, and they should be soft and sweet inside. Cook the croutons in the oil until they are golden brown on all sides.

For Herbal/Parmesan Croutons: Place the cooked croutons in a medium wooden bowl. Toss them with 1 teaspoon minced fresh Italian parsley, 1 teaspoon minced fresh rosemary, 1 teaspoon minced fresh thyme, and 4 tablespoons freshly grated Parmesan cheese.

For Spicy Croutons: Add 1 garlic clove, finely minced, and 3 chopped canned oil-cured anchovies to the pan filled with oil. Mash the anchovies into the oil, creating an anchovy oil. Cook the croutons in the oil. Place the croutons in a medium wooden bowl, and toss with ⅛ teaspoon cayenne pepper, 1 teaspoon cumin, 1 tablespoon minced fresh cilantro, and a dash of red pepper flakes.

Parmesan Crisps

These wafers look like pieces of lace but taste like crisp, buttery bits of Parmesan cheese. One is so light that after the initial bite it disappears in your mouth, leaving a wonderful, rich flavor behind.

4 teaspoons all-purpose flour
1 cup (about 4 ounces) finely grated Parmesan cheese
1 cup (about 4 ounces) finely grated Gruyère cheese
2 tablespoons unsalted butter, at room temperature
Cayenne pepper (optional)

Preheat the oven to 375°F.

Combine the ingredients. Cover a baking sheet with parchment paper. Drop 1 tablespoon of the mixture on the parchment paper. Using a spoon, spread into a 3- to 3½-inch oval. Repeat, spacing the ovals at 2- to 3-inch intervals.

Bake for 7 to 9 minutes, or until the crisps are golden. Make sure to check them after 4 minutes. Transfer to a rack to cool.

Makes 8 to 10 crisps

Spiced Nuts

As soon as you make these nuts, put them out of reach—otherwise you'll eat them all before you've sprinkled any over your salad. You can keep these for a couple of months in an airtight container in the refrigerator. Please feel free to use nuts that you most enjoy; just be conscious of their size when you're roasting them. Larger, denser nuts take longer to toast.

½ cup (2½ ounces) blanched, slivered almonds
½ cup (2 ounces) quartered walnuts
½ cup (about 2 ounces) raw *pepitas* (pumpkin seeds)
1 tablespoon olive oil
1 teaspoon sea salt
1 teaspoon ground cumin
1 teaspoon ground cinnamon
½ teaspoon cayenne pepper
Dash of allspice

Preheat the oven to 300°F. Toss the nuts in the oil. Spread them on a baking sheet, and roast until golden, about 10 to 12 minutes.

Toss the nuts with the rest of the ingredients.

Makes 2 cups

QUICK
VINAIGRETTES

VINAIGRETTES ARE PERHAPS THE MOST VERSATILE DRESSINGS.

Because of their thin texture, they are wonderful to use on salad greens and fresh vegetables. The more intensely flavored vinaigrettes like Oregano-Feta Vinaigrette and Avocado Vinaigrette work well with lighter pasta, rice, and potato salads and are equally delicious on fish, chicken, and beef. Many of the herbal and flavored vinaigrettes can be used as marinades for meat, fish, or vegetables. The vinegar and citrus base helps to tenderize the meat or vegetables and imparts a fresh, slightly tart flavor. Whether grilling or roasting, marinating adds an extra dimension to your food.

When using olive oil in vinaigrette recipes, always be sure to whisk until the oil is well blended with other ingredients.

Champagne Vinaigrette

This is an exceedingly delicate dressing, and so it should be paired with soft, fragile greens like mâche or watercress. It goes well with a salad that includes apples, pears, candied or spiced nuts, and mild cheeses.

1 teaspoon fresh lemon juice

1 shallot, minced

2 teaspoons Dijon mustard

¼ teaspoon sugar

4 teaspoons champagne vinegar

¾ cup extra-virgin olive oil

Sea salt and freshly ground
black pepper

In a medium bowl, combine the lemon juice, shallot, Dijon mustard, and sugar. With a fork, stir into a paste. Add the champagne vinegar. Whisk in the olive oil. Season with salt and pepper. Champagne Vinaigrette keeps refrigerated for up to 1 month.

MAKES 1 CUP

Raspberry Vinaigrette

This vinaigrette enhances the flavor of all fruits, including citrus, papayas, mangoes, berries, pears, and apples. It also pairs with headier, strong cheeses, such as Stilton, Gorgonzola, and shaved pecorino or Parmesan.

3 teaspoons raspberry vinegar

1 tablespoon orange zest

½ tablespoon honey

1 teaspoon minced fresh rosemary

¾ cup extra-virgin olive oil

Sea salt and freshly ground
black pepper

In a medium bowl, combine the raspberry vinegar, orange zest, honey, and rosemary. Whisk in the olive oil. Season with salt and pepper. Raspberry Vinaigrette keeps refrigerated for up to 1 month.

MAKES 1 CUP

Fresh Herbal Vinaigrette

This fresh, flavorful dressing goes well with tender greens, avocado, cucumber, tomatoes, and steamed new potatoes. It's also wonderful to use as a marinade for fish and chicken.

1 medium garlic clove, minced

1½ teaspoons Dijon mustard

Pinch of sugar

1 teaspoon minced fresh thyme

1 teaspoon minced fresh oregano

1 teaspoon minced fresh basil

1 teaspoon minced fresh mint

1½ teaspoons fresh lemon juice

3 teaspoons red wine

¾ cup extra-virgin olive oil

Sea salt and freshly ground
  black pepper

In a medium bowl, stir the garlic, Dijon mustard, and sugar with a fork, creating a paste. Add the fresh herbs, lemon juice, and red wine. Stir. Whisk in the olive oil. Season with salt and pepper. Fresh Herbal Vinaigrette keeps refrigerated for 1 week.

MAKES 1 CUP

Grapefruit Vinaigrette

Pair with a salad of escarole, avocado, and pieces of Ruby Red grapefruit!

1 shallot, minced

4 tablespoons fresh grapefruit juice

4 to 5 tablespoons champagne vinegar

1 teaspoon lime zest

1 teaspoon grapefruit zest

½ teaspoon honey

¾ cup extra-virgin olive oil

Sea salt and freshly ground
  black pepper

In a medium bowl, combine all the ingredients except the olive oil, salt, and pepper. Whisk in the olive oil. Season with salt and pepper. Grapefruit Vinaigrette keeps refrigerated for 2 weeks.

MAKES 1 CUP

Tangerine Vinaigrette

This vinaigrette has a tart yet sweet flavor. It goes very well with fish, shellfish, and flavorful vegetables such as fennel and steamed broccoli and asparagus.

2 teaspoons minced peeled fresh ginger

4 tablespoons fresh tangerine juice

1 teaspoon tangerine zest

1 tablespoon fresh lime juice

¼ teaspoon lime zest

3 tablespoons white wine vinegar

2 teaspoons minced fresh chives

¾ cup extra-virgin olive oil

Sea salt and freshly ground
  black pepper

In a medium bowl, combine all the ingredients except the olive oil, salt, and pepper. Whisk in the olive oil. Season with salt and pepper. Tangerine Vinaigrette keeps refrigerated for 2 weeks.

MAKES 1 CUP

Roasted Shallot–Sherry Vinaigrette

This rich vinaigrette is lovely on steamed vegetables like green beans, or a crisp frisée salad with a poached egg. The roasted shallots add a sweet flavor and smoky depth to the dressing.

8 shallots, peeled and ends trimmed

1 tablespoon olive oil

1 tablespoon whole-grain mustard

2 tablespoons sherry vinegar

1 teaspoon lemon zest

2 tablespoons coarsely chopped fresh parsley

¾ cup extra-virgin olive oil

Sea salt and freshly ground black pepper

Preheat the oven to 425°F.

In a small bowl, toss the shallots with the 1 tablespoon olive oil. Place the shallots in a pie tin, and roast them for 35 to 45 minutes, or until tender. Cool.

Put the mustard, vinegar, zest, and parsley into a blender or food processor fitted with a steel blade. Add 4 of the roasted shallots. Blend. Add the extra-virgin olive oil in a steady stream until the dressing emulsifies. Transfer to a medium bowl. Cut each of the remaining shallots in half, and add to the dressing. Season with salt and pepper. Roasted Shallot–Sherry Vinaigrette keeps refrigerated for 5 to 7 days.

MAKES 1 CUP

Tarragon Vinaigrette

The intense flavor of Tarragon dressing is wonderful with a very simple salad. It is lovely with a salad that has tomatoes.

1 shallot, minced

1 teaspoon Dijon mustard

Pinch of sugar

3 teaspoons fresh lemon juice

3 teaspoons tarragon or white
  wine vinegar

3 tablespoons chopped fresh tarragon

¾ cup virgin olive oil

Sea salt and freshly ground
  black pepper

In a medium bowl, combine all the ingredients except the olive oil, salt, and pepper. Whisk in the olive oil. Season with salt and pepper. Tarragon Vinaigrette keeps refrigerated for 2 weeks.

MAKES 1 CUP

Classic Dijon Vinaigrette

This hearty classic can be used on any kind of salad.

1 teaspoon balsamic vinegar

1 medium garlic clove, minced

3 teaspoons Dijon mustard

Pinch of sugar

3 teaspoons fresh lemon juice

Dash of Worcestershire sauce

1 teaspoon minced fresh thyme

¾ cup virgin olive oil

Sea salt and freshly ground
  black pepper

In a medium bowl, combine the balsamic vinegar, garlic, mustard, and sugar. With a fork, stir into a paste. Add the lemon juice, Worcestershire sauce, and thyme. Stir. Whisk in the olive oil. Season with salt and pepper. Classic Dijon Vinaigrette keeps refrigerated for 1 month.

MAKES 1 CUP

Salade Lyonnaise with Classic Dijon Vinaigrette

Here is my version of the famous French salad. A forkful of crisp frisée, sprinkled with small chunks of smoky bacon and dripping with egg yolk, is one of the great taste sensations.

2 heads of frisée	¼ cup white vinegar
2 teaspoons olive oil	4 eggs
8 extra-thick slices of apple-smoked bacon	4 tablespoons coarsely chopped fresh chives

Wash the frisée. Separate the washed leaves, and place them in a wooden salad bowl. Set aside.

In a medium cast-iron pan, heat the olive oil over medium heat. Place the bacon in the pan, and cook. Turn the bacon, making sure each slice is a deep golden brown but still has little bits of fat. Place the bacon on paper towels to drain.

Prepare the Classic Dijon Vinaigrette (page 21).

Dress the frisée with the vinaigrette. Place the dressed salad on 4 plates. Cut the bacon into small bite-size chunks.

Fill a medium saucepan with 2 inches of water. Add the vinegar, and bring to a boil. Crack the eggs delicately into the water. Let the eggs cook for 2 minutes, or until the yolks begin to solidify. With a slotted spoon, carefully pull each egg from the water, letting it drain before placing it on top of a plate of salad.

Garnish the poached eggs with the fresh chives. Sprinkle each salad with a generous amount of bacon. Serve.

SERVES 4

Avocado Vinaigrette

This dressing is so delicious that you may just want to eat it with a spoon and forget about tossing it with anything, although it's divine paired with Avocado Chicken Salad (see page 26). It's terrific to use as the dressing for any chicken or salmon salad or as an accompanying sauce to poached salmon or whitefish.

2 medium garlic cloves

1 teaspoon Dijon mustard

1½ teaspoons balsamic vinegar

2½ teaspoons fresh lemon juice

Dash of Worcestershire sauce

1 avocado, peeled, pitted, and
  sliced into quarters

Dash of cayenne pepper

½ teaspoon sea salt

¾ cup virgin olive oil

1 teaspoon lemon zest

Freshly ground black pepper

Put all the ingredients except the olive oil, zest, and black pepper into a blender or a food processor fitted with a steel blade. Blend. Add the olive oil in a steady stream until the dressing emulsifies. Transfer to a medium bowl. Fold the zest in with a large spoon. Season with pepper. Avocado Vinaigrette keeps refrigerated for 2 to 3 days.

MAKES 1 CUP

Avocado Chicken Salad with Avocado Vinaigrette

This creamy, savory salad may be one of the first dishes I ever created. It's wonderful with a glass of crisp, dry white wine on a hot summer day.

2½ cups chicken stock

1 whole chicken breast, bone in or out

2 cups mixed baby greens

½ avocado, cut into thin slices

½ medium jicama, cut into 3-inch chunks

½ red bell pepper, cut into thin slices

2 small Persian or Asian cucumbers, cut into thin slices

½ red onion, cut into thin slices

2 carrots, peeled and shredded

3 tablespoons olive oil

1 tablespoon balsamic vinegar

1 tablespoon fresh lemon juice

Sea salt and freshly ground black pepper

In a small saucepan, place the chicken stock and the chicken breast. Simmer the chicken breast in the stock for about 25 minutes. Check the chicken breast to confirm that the flesh is cooked to the bone. When the chicken is done, remove it from the bone, and shred. Set aside.

Make the Avocado Vinaigrette (page 24).

Put the chicken in a medium bowl. Toss with the dressing.

Combine the greens, avocado, jicama, bell pepper, cucumbers, onion, and carrots in a wooden salad bowl. Toss with the olive oil, balsamic vinegar, and lemon juice.

Place the mixed vegetables and greens on 4 dinner plates. Top each plate with a large scoop of the chicken mixture. Season with salt and pepper. Serve.

SERVES 4

Balsamic Vinaigrette

Balsamic vinegar has become a standard in many households. This dressing is delicious on any type of salad.

2 medium garlic cloves, minced

1 teaspoon Dijon mustard

3 tablespoons balsamic vinegar

1 teaspoon minced fresh thyme

¾ cup virgin olive oil

1 tablespoon orange zest

Sea salt and freshly ground
black pepper

In medium bowl, combine the garlic and Dijon mustard. Add the balsamic vinegar and minced thyme. Pour the olive oil in a steady stream, stirring with a whisk until emulsified. Add the zest. Season with salt and pepper. Balsamic Vinaigrette keeps refrigerated for 1 month.

MAKES 1 CUP

Stilton Cheese Vinaigrette

I adore this lighter blue cheese dressing, which is made with Stilton, a creamy, rich English blue cheese.

2 medium garlic cloves

1 tablespoon fresh lemon juice

3 tablespoons balsamic vinegar

¾ cup virgin olive oil

¼ cup (about 1 ounce) Stilton, crumbled

1 teaspoon lemon zest

Sea salt and freshly ground
black pepper

Combine the garlic, lemon juice, and balsamic vinegar in a blender or food processor fitted with a steel blade. Blend. Add the olive oil in a steady stream until the dressing emulsifies. Transfer to a medium bowl. Stir in the Stilton and zest. Season with salt and pepper. Stilton Cheese Vinaigrette keeps refrigerated for 3 to 5 days.

MAKES 1 CUP

Roasted Red Pepper Vinaigrette

I had this vinaigrette, served with toasted bread, at a restaurant in Los Angeles. It was so addicting that I thought I'd try to re-create it. Not only is it a lovely dipping sauce for bread, but it's also wonderful with a baby spinach salad smothered in feta, Greek olives, and toasted walnuts.

1 large red bell pepper	1 teaspoon sea salt
2 large garlic cloves	Dash of Tabasco sauce
2 teaspoons balsamic vinegar	¾ cup virgin olive oil
1 teaspoon fresh lemon juice	Freshly ground black pepper

Put the bell pepper on a fork and place it over a medium flame on the stove. When it blisters, turn it. Make sure all sides blister, and place it in a brown paper bag for 10 minutes. Cool.

Remove the pepper from the bag, and peel, halve, and core.

Put all the ingredients except the olive oil and black pepper into a blender or food processor fitted with a steel blade. Blend. Add the olive oil in a steady stream until the dressing emulsifies. Transfer to a medium bowl. Season with pepper. Roasted Red Pepper Vinaigrette keeps refrigerated for 2 weeks.

MAKES 1 CUP

Oregano-Feta Vinaigrette

This robust dressing is wonderful over a Greek salad or cucumber salad, or brushed over grilled lamb or steak. There are three types of feta: the Armenian cheese is the saltiest, the Greek is a tad less salty and a bit creamier, and the French is lightly salted and very creamy. Any of the three will work well in this dressing—choose the feta that you like best!

2 medium garlic cloves

1 tablespoon fresh lemon juice

3 tablespoons red wine vinegar

1 tablespoon dried oregano

½ cup (about 2½ ounces) crumbled feta

¾ cup virgin olive oil

1 tablespoon minced fresh oregano

Freshly ground black pepper

Combine all the ingredients except the olive oil, fresh oregano, and black pepper in a blender or food processor fitted with a steel blade. Mix. Add the olive oil in a steady stream until the dressing emulsifies. Transfer to a medium bowl. Add the fresh oregano. Season with pepper. Oregano-Feta Vinaigrette keeps refrigerated for 3 to 5 days.

MAKES 1 CUP

Classic Caesar Dressing

All you need is a few hearts of romaine, handfuls of crunchy homemade croutons, and several sprinklings of freshly grated Parmesan cheese—what a perfect salad! If you don't want to use the raw egg yolks in the dressing, substitute ½ tablespoon heavy cream and an additional tablespoon of Parmesan cheese.

Of course this dressing is perfect over a Classic Caesar, but I like to jazz it up with a little protein, such as poached chicken or fish, or—best of all—big, succulent shrimp.

3 medium garlic cloves

2 teaspoons Dijon mustard

4 tablespoons fresh lemon juice

2 egg yolks (see Note)

Dash of Worcestershire sauce

6 anchovy fillets, coarsely chopped

1 tablespoon freshly grated Parmesan cheese

¾ cup virgin olive oil

Freshly ground black pepper

Combine all the ingredients except the olive oil and black pepper in a blender or food processor fitted with a steel blade. Mix. Add the olive oil in a steady stream until the dressing emulsifies. Transfer to a medium bowl. Season with pepper. Classic Caesar Dressing keeps refrigerated for 5 to 7 days.

MAKES 1 CUP

Note:
Use refrigerated, sound-shelled, clean, fresh, grade AA or A eggs.

Classic Caesar with Shrimp

The crunch of the romaine combined with the salty, nutty flavor of Parmesan makes this a favorite salad for many. I include poached shrimp, which adds a little more heft and protein to the salad. This salad (pictured on page 33) is tossed with Classic Caesar Dressing.

1½ pounds uncooked large shrimp (24 to 28), peeled and deveined

1 teaspoon salt

1 head of romaine lettuce, outer leaves removed, inner leaves washed, dried, and torn into halves

½ cup (about 2 ounces) freshly grated Parmesan cheese

4 oil-packed anchovy fillets

Fill a large pot with water. Bring to a boil over medium-high heat. Add the shrimp and salt. Cook until the shrimp are opaque, about 2 to 3 minutes. Pull a shrimp from the pot, cut into the center to check that the shrimp is completely opaque. Drain the shrimp. Place in cold water to stop the cooking process.

Dry the shrimp.

Make the Classic Caesar Dressing (page 32).

In a large salad bowl, toss the romaine with the dressing. Add half of the Parmesan cheese. Toss again.

Place the salad on 4 dinner plates. Distribute the shrimp evenly over the greens. Sprinkle with the remaining Parmesan. Place an anchovy in the middle of each salad. Serve.

SERVES 4

Warm Bacon Vinaigrette

The bacon gives the dressing a wonderful smoky flavor and a nice crunchy bite. The warm dressing slowly wilts the leaves, creating a slightly tender yet still crisp texture. Because the dressing is warm, you want to drizzle your salad with the dressing seconds before you serve it, or the salad will become too saturated and soggy with dressing. I like this dressing best over spinach.

2 tablespoons plus ¾ cup virgin olive oil

6 slices of hickory- or
  apple-smoked bacon

3 medium shallots, coarsely chopped

1 tablespoon fresh lemon juice

3½ tablespoons red wine vinegar

1 teaspoon minced fresh oregano

1 teaspoon minced fresh thyme

Sea salt and freshly ground
  black pepper

Place a medium sauté pan or skillet over medium heat. Add 1 tablespoon olive oil. Heat for 2 minutes. Carefully add the bacon, using tongs to lay the slices flat in the pan. Cook for 8 to 10 minutes, until completely brown and crispy. Place the cooked bacon on paper towels to drain.

Place a small sauté pan or skillet over medium heat. Add 1 tablespoon olive oil. Heat for 1 minute. Add the shallots, and sauté 4 to 5 minutes, until translucent. Lower the heat, and add the lemon juice, red wine vinegar, oregano, and thyme. Heat for 1 to 2 minutes. Slowly add the ¾ cup olive oil. Heat for 2 minutes. Crumble the bacon and add it to the dressing. Season with salt and pepper. Serve immediately. Warm Bacon Vinaigrette keeps refrigerated for 3 to 5 days.

MAKES 1 CUP

Spinach Salad with Warm Bacon Vinaigrette

All you need with this salad is a loaf of warm crusty bread and a piece of Swiss Gruyère or Spanish manchego. If you can get interesting wild mushrooms at your local market, purchase an assortment, sauté them in 1 tablespoon of olive oil until soft, and add them to the salad.

4 cups baby spinach

10 white button mushrooms

5 shiitake mushrooms

½ medium red onion, peeled

½ fennel bulb

Wash and dry the spinach. Set aside.

Clean the white button and shiitake mushrooms with a damp paper towel. Slice off ⅛ inch from the bottom of each white button mushroom stem. Slice off the shiitake stems down to the mushroom top.

Cut the red onion into paper-thin slices. Take the outer leaf off the fennel bulb. Cut horizontally across the bulb, creating very thin slices.

Make the Warm Bacon Vinaigrette (page 35).

Place the spinach on 4 plates. Evenly divide the mushrooms, red onion, and fennel among them. Spoon several tablespoons of the dressing over each plate. Serve immediately.

SERVES 4

CREAMY
CREATIONS

vegetables; they cover them. To me, creamy dressings are the meat loaf or turkey dinners of salad dressings—they say "comfort food."

In this section, you'll find 12 foolproof dressings that will add a soft, savory flavor to your rice, potato, or roasted vegetable salad. Many of these dressings are also wonderful when used as dips or as sauces with fish or meat.

The recipes range from American classics like Blue Cheese Dressing to spicy Spanish *Romesco* Sauce.

Tangy Buttermilk-Horseradish Dressing

This is a version of Deborah Madison's recipe for this wonderful dressing. Try this rich, creamy dressing laced with horseradish on your baked potato, instead of butter or sour cream. I also love it with shredded cabbage, or over a big chunk of iceberg lettuce with a few bits of crispy bacon on top.

½ cup buttermilk

½ cup sour cream

1½ tablespoons prepared horseradish

2 medium garlic cloves

1½ tablespoons fresh lemon juice

½ cup coarsely chopped fresh Italian parsley

Pinch of sugar

1 teaspoon lemon zest

Salt and freshly ground black pepper

Combine all the ingredients except the zest, salt, and pepper in a blender or food processor fitted with a steel blade. Blend until smooth. Transfer to a medium bowl. Add the zest, and stir. Season with salt and pepper. Tangy Buttermilk-Horseradish Dressing keeps refrigerated for 5 to 7 days.

MAKES 1 CUP

Roasted Vegetable Salad with Tangy Buttermilk-Horseradish Dressing

Not only is this salad beautiful, but it's also simple and delicious. It's a perfect side dish for any entrée and a wonderful addition to a group of vegetarian dishes. If some vegetables aren't available, feel free to substitute.

4 large bunches of watercress

2 to 3 small red onions, quartered

2 red bell peppers, stemmed, seeded, and cut into 1-inch strips

1 yellow bell pepper, stemmed, seeded, and cut into 1-inch strips

6 parsnips, peeled, halved, and cut into thirds

1 head of broccolini, separated and with ½ inch trimmed from the bottom

3 small Yukon Gold potatoes, cut into quarters

2 small heads of radicchio, cut into quarters

5 medium garlic cloves

3 tablespoons olive oil, plus more for drizzling as needed

½ teaspoon sea salt

Freshly ground black pepper

⅓ cup coarsely chopped fresh Italian parsley

Clean and dry the watercress. Pull off the long stems. Roll up in a slightly damp paper towel, and place in a plastic bag in the refrigerator.

Preheat the oven to 450°F.

In a large bowl, toss the vegetables and garlic with the 3 tablespoons olive oil and sea salt. Season with black pepper.

Place the vegetables in a large roasting pan. If the mixture seems dry, drizzle with a little additional olive oil. Roast for 1 hour, or until browned and crisp around the edges.

Put the watercress on a large decorative platter. Place the roasted vegetables on top.

Make the Tangy Buttermilk-Horseradish Dressing (page 39).

Spoon the dressing generously over the vegetables. Garnish with the Italian parsley. Serve.

SERVES 4

Green Goddess Dressing

This gorgeous green dressing popped onto the food scene in the 1970s—thus its slightly hippie name. It's wonderful over a salad full of crunchy vegetables or used as a sauce with poached fish or chicken.

½ cup mayonnaise

½ cup sour cream

1½ tablespoons tarragon vinegar

1½ tablespoons fresh lemon juice

2 garlic cloves, minced

½ cup chopped fresh Italian parsley

1 tablespoon chopped fresh mint

1½ tablespoons chopped fresh tarragon

2 tablespoons chopped fresh chives

6 anchovy fillets, coarsely chopped

Salt and freshly ground black pepper

Combine all the ingredients except the salt and pepper in a blender or food processor fitted with a steel blade. Blend until completely smooth. Transfer to a medium bowl. Season with salt and pepper. Green Goddess Dressing keeps refrigerated for 5 to 7 days.

MAKES 1 CUP

Thousand Island Dressing

Slather your burger bun with this classic American dressing or dip your steamed shrimp into this mixture—Thousand Island is best homemade.

1 shallot, minced

½ cup mayonnaise

3 tablespoons ketchup

2 tablespoons cider vinegar

2 teaspoons chopped sweet pickles

1 tablespoon capers

Dash of Worcestershire sauce

Salt and freshly ground black pepper
   to taste

1 lemon, halved (optional)

Combine all the ingredients in a medium bowl. Stir well. Add a squeeze of lemon juice if the dressing seems too sweet. Thousand Island Dressing keeps refrigerated for 5 to 7 days.

MAKES 1 CUP

Russian Dressing

In my house, when I was growing up my family didn't rely on Thousand Island —we had Russian dressing. The two are quite similar, but Russian dressing tends to be less sweet and a bit more tart. I love to use it as a dipping sauce for raw cauliflower and endive.

1 shallot, minced

½ cup mayonnaise

3 tablespoons ketchup

1 tablespoon fresh lemon juice

1 tablespoon white wine vinegar

½ teaspoon prepared horseradish

Dash of Tabasco sauce

Dash of Worcestershire sauce

Salt and freshly ground black pepper
   to taste

Combine all the ingredients in a medium bowl. Stir well. Russian Dressing keeps refrigerated for 5 to 7 days.

MAKES 1 CUP

Creamy Dill Dressing

This yogurt-based dressing is lovely spooned over poached fish.

½ cup plain yogurt

1 tablespoon buttermilk

2 tablespoons cider vinegar

½ tablespoon fresh lemon juice

2 garlic cloves, minced

½ cup chopped fresh dill

1 teaspoon honey

Dash of cayenne pepper

2 tablespoons capers

1 tablespoon lemon zest

Salt and freshly ground black pepper

Combine all the ingredients except the capers, zest, salt, and black pepper in a blender or food processor fitted with a steel blade. Blend until creamy and smooth. Transfer to a medium bowl. Stir in the capers and zest. Season with salt and pepper. Creamy Dill Dressing keeps refrigerated for 5 to 7 days.

MAKES 1 CUP

Ranch Dressing

Try Ranch Dressing with your favorite mixture of delicate and crunchy vegetables.

½ cup mayonnaise

¼ cup plain yogurt

¼ cup milk

1 teaspoon Dijon mustard

1 teaspoon dried basil

1 teaspoon fresh lemon juice

1 teaspoon white wine vinegar

Pinch of sugar

Salt and freshly ground black pepper

Combine all the ingredients except the salt and pepper in a blender or food processor fitted with a steel blade. Blend until smooth. Transfer to a medium bowl. Season with salt and pepper. Ranch Dressing keeps refrigerated for 5 to 7 days.

MAKES 1 CUP

Dijon Cream Dressing

This dressing is delicious over steamed or roasted vegetables. I love to use it as the dressing for a potato and a fresh steamed-mussel salad (see page 48).

1 shallot, minced	1 tablespoon chopped fresh dill
1½ tablespoons Dijon mustard	1 teaspoon lemon zest
¾ cup sour cream	2 teaspoons fresh lemon juice
2 tablespoons heavy (whipping) cream	Dash of Worcestershire sauce
1 tablespoon tarragon vinegar	Salt and freshly ground black pepper

Combine all the ingredients except the salt and pepper in a medium bowl. Stir until smooth. Season with salt and pepper. Dijon Cream Dressing keeps refrigerated for 5 to 7 days.

MAKES 1 CUP

Blue Cheese Dressing

Ah, blue cheese! This decadent dressing is divine spooned over any dense, crunchy lettuce, and it is wonderful as a dip for fresh, crisp vegetables.

6 tablespoons virgin olive oil	Dash of Worcestershire sauce
6 tablespoons sour cream or plain yogurt	½ cup (about 2 ounces) blue cheese (drier blue cheese, e.g. Point Reyes), crumbled
2 medium garlic cloves	
3 tablespoons sherry vinegar	Salt and freshly ground black pepper

Combine all the ingredients except the blue cheese, salt, and pepper in a medium bowl. Slowly add the blue cheese, mixing some pieces of cheese into the dressing and leaving some bigger chunks to give it a nice lumpy texture. Season with salt and pepper. Blue Cheese Dressing keeps refrigerated for 5 to 7 days.

MAKES 1 CUP

Dijon Cream Potato Salad with Steamed Mussels and Green Beans

I first had a version of this Mark Bittman salad years ago, and have been making my own interpretation ever since. The plump, slightly chewy mussels are mixed with soft, waxy potatoes and finished off with the fresh, clean taste of string beans; the combination makes this a perfect main-course salad for lunch or dinner. It's important to use small, waxy tubers like white rose or new potatoes, not large, fluffy ones like Idaho potatoes. This salad is best when combined with the Dijon Cream Dressing on page 47.

3 pounds black mussels

½ teaspoon sea salt

1 lemon, halved

1½ pounds small new potatoes
(each the size of a golf ball)

1 pound small green beans

Salt and freshly ground black pepper

2 tablespoons coarsely chopped
fresh chives

Clean the mussels. Make sure to pull the beards and scrape the barnacles off.

In a large pot, bring 2 cups of water to a boil over medium heat. Add the salt and lemon. Add the cleaned mussels, cover, and steam for 8 to 10 minutes. Cook until the mussels open, shaking the pot every couple of minutes. Pull the opened mussels from the pot and let cool. Take the mussel meat out of the shells, and discard the shells.

Peel and cut the potatoes in half. Place the potatoes in a large pot with 3 cups of water. Bring to a boil over medium heat, cover, and cook for 8 to 10 minutes, or until tender. Strain in cold water. Set aside.

In a steamer, place 2 inches of water. Bring to a boil over medium heat. Place the beans in the steamer, and cook for 3 minutes, or until tender but still crisp. Strain in cold water immediately. Set aside.

Make the Dijon Cream Dressing (page 47).

In a large bowl, combine the mussels, potatoes, and green beans. Lightly toss with the Dijon Cream Dressing until all the ingredients are coated. Season with salt and pepper. Garnish with the fresh chives. Serve.

SERVES 4

Cilantro Cream Dressing

Add this creamy, bold dressing to a fish taco. Spoon it over a pile of steamed broccoli or asparagus. Or, spread it on a roast beef sandwich.

1 cup sour cream

3 tablespoons virgin olive oil

3 tablespoons fresh lime juice

1 tablespoon fresh orange juice

2 medium garlic cloves, minced

1 small serrano chile, stemmed, seeded, and diced

½ cup chopped fresh cilantro

Salt

Combine all the ingredients except the salt in a blender or food processor fitted with a steel blade. Blend until creamy and smooth. Transfer to a medium bowl. Season with salt. Cilantro Cream Dressing keeps refrigerated for 5 to 7 days.

MAKES 1 CUP

Tropical Cream Dressing

Toss this tangy, sweet dressing into a fruit salad of berries or tropical fruits.

1 cup plain yogurt

1 ripe mango

¼ teaspoon pure vanilla extract

¼ teaspoon pure almond extract

2 tablespoons honey

2 tablespoons fresh lime juice

1 tablespoon fresh orange juice

1 tablespoon orange zest

2 tablespoons chopped fresh mint

Combine all the ingredients except the zest and mint in a blender or food processor fitted with a steel blade. Blend until smooth. Transfer to a medium bowl. Add the zest and mint, and stir. Tropical Cream Dressing keeps refrigerated for 5 to 7 days.

MAKES 1 CUP

Grapefruit Mayonnaise

This flavored mayonnaise is wonderful when it is spooned or spread on any poultry or fish—think salmon, turkey, tuna, or smoked trout. It's also fabulous used in a sandwich.

1 large egg

1½ teaspoons Dijon mustard

1 cup virgin olive oil

2 teaspoons fresh lemon juice

4 teaspoons fresh grapefruit juice

Dash of Worcestershire sauce

½ teaspoon sea salt

1½ teaspoons finely grated grapefruit zest

Freshly ground black pepper

In a blender or food processor fitted with a steel blade, combine the egg and Dijon mustard with ½ cup of the olive oil. Blend at low speed. With the motor running, add the remaining olive oil in a steady stream. Add the remaining ingredients except the zest and pepper and pulse 4 to 6 times until blended.

Transfer to a medium bowl. Stir in the zest. Season with pepper. Grapefruit Mayonnaise keeps refrigerated for 5 to 7 days.

MAKES 1 CUP

Poached Salmon with Grapefruit Mayonnaise

I like to serve the fish over a bed of mâche accompanied by thin slices of avocado, red onion, and Persian or Japanese cucumber. The poached salmon (pictured on page 53) goes particularly well with the Grapefruit Mayonnaise dressing, a twist on the traditional hollandaise.

COURT BOUILLON

2 bay leaves

6 sprigs fresh Italian parsley

1 sprig fresh thyme

2 celery tops with leaves

6 peppercorns, bruised

½ bottle dry white wine

1 carrot, peeled and chopped

1 small red onion, quartered

½ tablespoon sea salt

Juice of 1 lemon

1 two-pound fillet salmon

6 cups mâche, cleaned

1 Hass avocado, peeled, pitted, and cut into thin slices

½ small red onion, cut into thin slices

2 Persian or Japanese cucumbers, cut into thin slices

To prepare the court bouillon: Make a bouquet garni by tying the herbs, celery, and peppercorns in a square of cheesecloth. In a large saucepan, combine the wine, carrot, quartered red onion, salt, lemon juice, 4 cups water, and the bouquet garni. Bring to a simmer over medium-low heat, and cook for 30 to 35 minutes. Remove from the heat and let cool. Strain into a container and set aside.

Rinse the fish. Place in a medium pan. Pour the strained cooled court bouillon over the fish to cover. If more liquid is needed, add water.

Place the pan over medium-low heat. Cover, and cook for 30 minutes.

Make the Grapefruit Mayonnaise (page 52).

Using 2 spatulas, carefully remove the fish from the pan. Remove the skin. With a dull knife, scrape any residue of gray skin from the pink salmon flesh.

On a decorative platter, place the mâche evenly. Lay the fish on top of the mâche; alternately, around the fish, place the avocado, onion slices, and cucumbers. Spoon some of the dressing down the middle of the fish, and put the rest in a small bowl and serve on the side.

SERVES 4

Romesco Sauce

This Catalonian sauce is a mixture of tomatoes, chiles, roasted red bell peppers, hazelnuts, and almonds. It's typically served with seafood and poultry, but it's also wonderful with lamb, beef, or roasted or grilled pork (see page 56). I also use it as a tangy spread on a rustic sandwich.

4 tablespoons (about 1 ounce) almonds

2 tablespoons hazelnuts

½ ancho chile

1½-inch-thick slice of stale crusty bread

2 teaspoons plus ½ cup virgin olive oil

4 medium garlic cloves, minced

½ cup coarsely chopped canned peeled tomatoes

4 tablespoons coarsely chopped roasted red bell peppers or pimientos

2 tablespoons sherry vinegar

2 anchovy fillets, minced

Dash of cayenne pepper

1 teaspoon orange zest

Preheat the broiler.

In a small baking dish, place the almonds and hazelnuts. Toast the nuts for 5 to 7 minutes, or until golden brown. Set aside to cool.

Soak the chile in ¼ cup of boiling water for about 4 minutes. Once it is soft, pat it dry, cut off the stem, and seed. Set aside.

Brush the bread with the 2 teaspoons olive oil, put it under the broiler, and toast 1 minute per side, until golden on both sides.

In a blender or food processor fitted with a steel blade, combine all the ingredients except the cayenne pepper and zest. Blend until smooth. (If you prefer a little texture, blend until just shy of smooth, leaving a few bits of nuts and tiny bread crusts in the mixture.) Transfer to a medium bowl. Stir in the cayenne pepper, and check the heat of the sauce. It should be spicy but not overwhelming. Fold in the zest. If the dressing seems too thick, add 1 to 2 tablespoons of water. *Romesco* Sauce keeps refrigerated for 5 to 7 days.

MAKES 1 CUP

Rib-eye Steak Salad with *Romesco* Sauce

I like to lay the sliced steak on a bed of chopped escarole laced with thin slices of red onions, avocados, and golden and orange bell peppers. It's also delicious served on a bed of roasted asparagus. The salad goes wonderfully with the tangy *Romesco* Sauce.

2 heads of escarole

½ medium red onion, thinly sliced

1 large Hass avocado, peeled, pitted, and cut lengthwise into thin slices

1 orange bell pepper, stemmed, seeded, and cut lengthwise into thin slices

1 yellow bell pepper, stemmed, seeded, and cut lengthwise into thin slices

4 tablespoons olive oil

1 tablespoon balsamic vinegar

4 eight-ounce rib-eye steaks

2 tablespoons sea salt

Freshly ground black pepper

Wash the escarole, discarding any tough outer leaves. Dry and chop the escarole into 2-inch pieces.

Make the *Romesco* Sauce (page 55).

Place the chopped escarole, red onion, avocado, and bell peppers in a salad bowl. Toss with 2 tablespoons of the olive oil and the balsamic vinegar.

Brush the steaks with the remaining 2 tablespoons olive oil, and sprinkle with the sea salt. Place a large, heavy cast-iron sauté pan or skillet over medium-high heat. Add two steaks at a time to the pan, and cook 3 minutes on each side for medium-rare. Place on a carving board. Repeat with the remaining 2 steaks. Let stand for 5 minutes. Slice the steaks into thin strips. Season with pepper.

Toss the salad again. Place it on a large decorative platter. Arrange the pieces of steak on top, and generously drizzle over some of the *Romesco* Sauce. Serve the rest of the *Romesco* Sauce on the side.

SERVES 4

FABULOUS
FLAVORS

YOU MIGHT BE THINKING, "AREN'T ALL THE DRESSINGS INCLUDED in this book full of fabulous flavor? What makes the dressings in this chapter different?" The answer is simple: They are influenced by a variety of cultures. The ingredients may not be ones that we eat regularly, but they are readily available— think miso, *pepitas,* or *ponzu.*

These dressings are as versatile as others in the book. In each recipe introduction, I've made sure to offer what is best paired with each particular recipe.

Creamy Cucumber-Mint Yogurt Dressing

The Greeks have a version called *tzatziki;* the Indians have a version they call *raita.* It's terrific as a side dish with fish, chicken, or lamb. You can also use it as a dip with raw, steamed, roasted, or grilled vegetables. One of my favorite things to do is to grill or roast slices of eggplant with a little olive oil and then slather them with this creamy, crunchy dressing.

¾ cup plain yogurt

1 Persian or Japanese cucumber, cut into thin slices

2 medium garlic cloves, minced

3 tablespoons coarsely chopped fresh mint

1 tablespoon white wine vinegar

1 teaspoon fresh lemon juice

¼ teaspoon sea salt

Freshly ground black pepper to taste

In a medium bowl, combine all the ingredients. Taste and add more salt if needed. Creamy Cucumber-Mint Yogurt Dressing keeps refrigerated for 5 to 7 days.

MAKES 1 CUP

Thai Lime Dressing

With its tart, slightly sweet flavor, this dressing is best with dumplings or fried vegetables, fish, or shrimp. I like to fry a few shrimp, roll each in a lettuce leaf, and then dip the bundle into this tangy sauce.

Juice of 4 to 5 limes

2 tablespoons sesame oil

1 tablespoon soy sauce

4 tablespoons fish sauce (nuoc mam)

1½ tablespoons sugar

1 serrano chile, stemmed, halved, seeded, and cut into thin quarter moons

2 tablespoons minced fresh mint

In a medium bowl, combine all the ingredients. Thai Lime Dressing keeps refrigerated for 5 to 7 days.

MAKES 1 CUP

Broiled Calamari Salad with Thai Lime Dressing

This is a wonderful, refreshing salad to enjoy in the hot summer months. Try to buy your squid cleaned. You can often find cleaned squid in your market freezer or fresh and frozen at your fish market. This Asian-inspired recipe is especially good with the tart Thai Lime Dressing.

1½ pounds cleaned squid

1 tablespoon olive oil

Sea salt and freshly ground black pepper

1½ cups baby lettuce, washed

1 Hass avocado, peeled, pitted, and cut lengthwise into thin slices

1½ Persian or Japanese cucumbers, cut into thin slices

½ small red onion, cut into thin slices

½ large papaya, peeled, seeded, and cut into large bite-size pieces

1½ tablespoons coarsely chopped fresh mint

Make the Thai Lime Dressing (page 59).

Preheat the broiler.

Leaving the tentacles intact, cut the squid into rings. In a medium bowl, toss the squid with the olive oil and salt and pepper. Spread the rings on one baking sheet and the tentacles on another.

In a salad bowl, combine the remaining ingredients except the mint.

Place the two baking sheets under the broiler. Broil the squid rings for 1 to 2 minutes, and broil the tentacles for 2 to 3 minutes. Check the rings and tentacles after 1 minute. If they cook too long, they will be very chewy. They should be tender and succulent.

Using a slotted spoon, transfer the squid to the salad. Toss the salad with the Thai Lime Dressing. Place the salad on a serving plate. Garnish with the mint and serve.

SERVES 4

Creamy Coconut Dressing

I've had this dressing over jasmine rice and topped with toasted coconut. It's also wonderful with a fruit salad of mangoes, papayas, and berries.

¾ cup plain yogurt

¼ cup unsweetened coconut milk

1½ teaspoons honey

2 to 3 tablespoons fresh lime juice

2 to 3 tablespoons dried, unsweetened coconut

½ teaspoon ground cumin

¼ teaspoon sea salt

2 tablespoons minced fresh mint

In a medium bowl, combine all the ingredients. Creamy Coconut Dressing keeps refrigerated for 5 to 7 days.

MAKES 1 CUP

Roasted Sesame–Soy Dressing

I enjoy this nutty dressing over steamed snow peas, bok choy, or baby broccoli. It's also a wonderful marinade for duck or chicken.

3 tablespoons sesame seeds

2 medium garlic cloves, minced

1 tablespoon minced peeled fresh ginger

3 tablespoons rice wine vinegar

2 tablespoons soy sauce

1 tablespoon honey

¼ cup canola oil

3 tablespoons sesame oil

Preheat the oven to 425°F.

In a pie tin, place the sesame seeds. Place in the middle of the upper shelf of the oven. Toast the seeds for 4 minutes, or until golden brown. Cool.

Combine all the ingredients in a blender or food processor fitted with a steel blade. Blend until smooth. Roasted Sesame Soy Dressing keeps refrigerated for 5 to 7 days.

MAKES 1 CUP

Thai Peanut Dressing

I serve this over buckwheat noodles with shredded cucumbers and chicken.

4 tablespoons crunchy peanut butter

1 tablespoon hoisin sauce

¼ cup canola oil

2 medium garlic cloves, minced

2 tablespoons minced peeled fresh ginger

¼ teaspoon cayenne pepper

6 tablespoons rice wine vinegar

3 scallions, minced

Combine all the ingredients except the scallions in a blender or food processor fitted with a steel blade. Blend until smooth. Add the scallions, and stir.

MAKES 1 CUP

Roasted *Pepitas* and Chipotle Dressing

This exotic dressing is excellent over crisp vegetables and greens or spooned over fish, poultry, or pork. It keeps refrigerated for 5 to 7 days.

2 medium garlic cloves, unpeeled

4 tablespoons *pepitas* (pumpkin seeds)

Juice of 1 lime

½ pound tomatillos (about 7) husked and quartered

½ teaspoon sugar

½ teaspoon salt

2 tablespoons minced fresh cilantro

½ cup canola oil

Dash of cayenne pepper

Preheat the oven to 425°F.

In a pie tin, place the garlic cloves, with the skins on, on the upper shelf of the oven. Roast for 15 minutes. Cool. Peel. In another pie tin, place the *pepitas* on the upper shelf of the oven. Roast for 6 to 8 minutes.

Combine all the ingredients in a blender or food processor fitted with a steel blade. Blend until smooth.

MAKES 1 CUP

Shredded Cucumber, Buckwheat Noodle, and Poached Chicken Salad with Thai Peanut Dressing

Whenever I see this salad (pictured on page 65) on a restaurant menu, I've got to get it. It blends all the best tastes and textures in one dish. This salad is traditionally served with a Thai Peanut Dressing.

2½ cups chicken stock

Splash of fish sauce (you can substitute a little rice wine vinegar and ½ teaspoon anchovy paste)

1 whole chicken breast, bone in or out

5 tablespoons (about 2 ounces) peanuts, chopped

1 pound buckwheat noodles

1 large cucumber, peeled

1 tablespoon rice wine vinegar (optional)

In a small saucepan, place the chicken stock, fish sauce, and the chicken breast. Simmer over low heat for 25 to 30 minutes. Check the chicken breast to confirm that the flesh is cooked through. When the chicken is done and cool enough to handle, shred it and set aside.

Preheat the oven to 425°F.

In a pie tin, place the peanuts. Place in the middle of the upper shelf of the oven. Roast for 6 to 8 minutes, or until golden brown. Cool.

Make the Thai Peanut Dressing (page 64).

Fill a stockpot with water, and bring to a boil over medium-high heat. Add the buckwheat noodles and cook according to the package's instructions. Rinse the noodles in cool water. Set aside.

In a blender or food processor fitted with a shredder blade, shred the cucumber. Drain in a colander. Set aside.

In a large bowl, combine all the ingredients, reserving 3 tablespoons of the roasted peanuts. Toss the salad with the Thai Peanut Dressing. Taste, and if it needs an extra kick, add the rice wine vinegar. Toss again. Place the salad on a serving platter. Garnish with the 3 tablespoons roasted peanuts and serve.

SERVES 4

Bagna Cauda

This dip's name comes from the Italian term *bagno caldo,* or "hot bath." The sauce originated in the Piedmont region of northern Italy. It's wonderful as a dip for raw vegetables or drizzled over fish or sliced roasted chicken.

12 to 14 anchovy fillets, chopped	2 tablespoons unsalted butter
4 medium garlic cloves, minced	1 tablespoon fresh lemon juice
¾ cup virgin olive oil	1 tablespoon lemon zest

In a small saucepan, place the anchovies, garlic, and olive oil over low heat. Cook, whisking continuously, until the flavors meld together, 5 to 10 minutes. Whisk in the butter until the mixture becomes creamy. Add the lemon juice and zest. Whisk once more. Serve in a fondue pot to keep the sauce warm. *Bagna Cauda* keeps refrigerated for 5 to 7 days.

MAKES 1 CUP

Ginger-*Ponzu* Dressing

The lemon flavor of the *ponzu* and the slight heat of the ginger give this light dressing a lot of punch. It's wonderful with Asian greens like mizuna (see page 69), or as a marinade for fleshy whitefish.

4 tablespoons *ponzu*	2 tablespoons rice wine vinegar
2 tablespoons soy sauce	3 tablespoons sesame oil
1½ tablespoons minced peeled fresh ginger	1½ teaspoons honey
	2 tablespoons minced fresh cilantro

In a medium bowl combine all the ingredients. Whisk until the ingredients are well blended. Ginger-*Ponzu* Dressing keeps refrigerated for 5 to 7 days.

MAKES 1 CUP

Tuna Tartare Salad with Ginger-*Ponzu* Dressing

Buy the best sashimi-grade tuna you can find. It's important that it be sashimi grade for both your health and the taste of the fish. I like to serve this salad with very dry, thin crackers. The lemon flavor of the *ponzu* mixed with ginger complements the richness of the tuna.

1 tablespoon sesame seeds

1½ pounds sashimi-grade tuna steak

3 scallions, cut into thin slices

Juice of ½ lemon

3 cups mâche, mizuna, or watercress

1 Hass avocado, peeled, pitted, and cut into thin slices

Preheat the oven to 425°F.

In a pie tin, place the sesame seeds on the upper shelf of the oven and toast them for 5 minutes, or until golden. Cool.

On a chopping board, mince the tuna steak. Place it in a medium bowl. Add the scallions and lemon juice. Mix with a fork, making sure that the scallions are evenly blended with the fish.

Make the Ginger-*Ponzu* Dressing (page 67).

Slowly add ½ cup of the dressing and see if the tuna is flavorful enough. Add more dressing until the tuna has a lot of flavor and a nice spreadable texture.

Dry the mâche, mizuna, or watercress. Divide the greens among 4 salad plates. Put a large scoop of the tuna tartare on top of each plate of greens. Surround each scoop of tartare with slices of avocado. Garnish with the toasted sesame seeds. Serve.

SERVES 4

Indian Curry Dressing

This slightly spicy dressing can be used as a marinade for chicken or lamb, as well as a sauce for dipping vegetables or for topping steamed or roasted new potatoes.

¾ cup plain yogurt

1 teaspoon honey

2 tablespoons fresh lime juice

2 medium garlic cloves, minced

2 tablespoons coarsely chopped
   fresh cilantro

½ teaspoon ground cumin

1 teaspoon curry powder

¼ teaspoon salt

Dash of cayenne pepper

In a medium bowl, combine all the ingredients. Taste and add more salt if needed. Indian Curry Dressing keeps refrigerated for 5 to 7 days.

MAKES 1 CUP

Tahini Dressing

The creamy sesame paste lends both a depth and full, buttery flavor to this Middle Eastern–inspired dressing. Tahini goes well with nearly everything. It's divine with roasted or raw vegetables, and it's equally delicious drizzled over lamb or chicken.

2 medium garlic cloves, minced

4 tablespoons tahini

6 tablespoons canola oil

3 tablespoons fresh lemon juice

2 tablespoons fresh Italian parsley,
   minced

Salt and freshly ground black pepper

In a medium bowl, combine all the ingredients and 3 tablespoons of water. To thin the sauce, add 1 to 2 tablespoons of water. Tahini Dressing keeps refrigerated for 5 to 7 days.

MAKES 1 CUP

Lime, Tequila, and Cilantro Dressing

The addition of tequila gives this dressing a nice edge. It's wonderful as a marinade for a whitefish like black cod or for a heartier, meaty fish like swordfish. I also love to use it as a dressing for shredded cabbage, which I stuff inside a tortilla with a little roasted chicken and guacamole for a perfect dinner or snack.

5 tablespoons fresh lime juice

2 tablespoons fresh grapefruit juice

¾ cup virgin olive oil

4 tablespoons finely chopped
  fresh cilantro

1 medium garlic clove, minced

3 teaspoons tequila

½ teaspoon sugar

¼ teaspoon sea salt

1 small serrano chile, stemmed,
  seeded, and minced

In a medium bowl, combine all the ingredients except the serrano chile. Add the chile a little at a time until the dressing reaches the desired level of spiciness. Lime, Tequila, and Cilantro Dressing keeps refrigerated for 5 to 7 days.

MAKES 1 CUP

Spicy Mexican Black Bean Dressing

Spoon this full-bodied, flavorful dressing over poultry or pork. It's also divine slathered on top of a baked potato and topped with a dollop of sour cream. If you use a little less oil and puree only half of the beans, it makes a wonderful salsa.

2 red bell peppers

½ fifteen-ounce can of black beans, drained

Juice of 1 lime

2 tablespoons sherry vinegar

¼ jalapeño chile, stemmed, seeded, and coarsely chopped

½ cup virgin olive oil

¼ teaspoon salt, plus more for seasoning (optional)

2 teaspoons orange zest

Pierce the red bell pepper with a fork. Hold the bell pepper above a medium flame until it begins to blister. Repeat on all sides. Repeat with the remaining bell pepper.

Place the roasted bell peppers in a brown paper bag. Close the bag for 5 minutes. Shake the peppers gently. Peel, halve, and seed. Cut into 1-inch strips.

Combine all the ingredients except the orange zest in a blender or food processor fitted with a steel blade. Blend until smooth. Transfer to a medium bowl. Add the orange zest. Season with salt if needed. If the dressing seems too thick, add 1 to 2 tablespoons of water. Spicy Mexican Black Bean Dressing keeps refrigerated for 5 to 7 days.

MAKES 1 CUP

Creamy Fig-Mint Dressing

Is it a dessert or is it a dressing? Good question. If you forget the olive oil and add a dozen sliced fresh figs, you could call it dessert, but this version is a dressing. I've even used it as an accompaniment for lamb or roast chicken. It's also fabulous over poached pears, or in a fall fruit salad of figs, pears, and apples with a few sections of blood orange thrown in for tang and color.

8 fresh Black Mission figs or
  6 dried figs

2 tablespoons balsamic vinegar

1 tablespoon fresh lemon juice

½ cup plain yogurt

3 tablespoons virgin olive oil

3 tablespoons minced fresh mint

Dash of finely ground black pepper

1 scant tablespoon orange zest

If you are using dried figs, place them in a small, heat-proof bowl, and cover with boiling water. Let soak for 20 to 25 minutes until the figs are plump and soft.

Cut the figs into fourths.

Combine all the ingredients except the zest in a blender or food processor fitted with a steel blade. Blend until smooth. Transfer to a medium bowl. Add the zest. Stir until fully blended. Creamy Fig-Mint Dressing keeps refrigerated for 5 to 7 days.

MAKES 1 CUP

Asian Pear, Endive, and Roasted Walnut Salad with Creamy Fig-Mint Dressing

I love to serve this salad with a roasted pork shoulder or roast beef. It's elegant enough to serve as a course for a dinner party, and easy enough to prepare whenever you're in the mood for a crunchy, slightly sweet, and slightly bitter salad. The Creamy Fig-Mint Dressing is the perfect complement to this sweet and savory salad.

½ cup (2 ounces) walnut halves

8 heads of washed Belgian endive, cored, and quartered lengthwise

2 Asian pears, cored and thinly sliced, or 2 Fuyu persimmons, peeled, cored, and thinly sliced

Preheat the oven to 425°F.

Place the walnuts in a pie tin, and roast them for 5 to 7 minutes, or until golden. Cool.

Make the Creamy Fig-Mint Dressing (page 75).

In a salad bowl, combine the endive, Asian pears, and half the toasted walnuts. Toss with the dressing.

Place the salad on 4 salad plates, and evenly divide the remaining walnuts, sprinkling them over each plate. Serve.

SERVES 4

INDEX

TABLE OF EQUIVALENTS

The exact equivalents in the following table have been rounded for convenience.

LIQUID/DRY MEASURES

U.S.	METRIC
¼ teaspoon	1.25 milliliters
½ teaspoon	2.5 milliliters
1 teaspoon	5 milliliters
1 tablespoon (3 teaspoons)	15 milliliters
1 fluid ounce (2 tablespoons)	30 milliliters
¼ cup	60 milliliters
⅓ cup	80 milliliters
½ cup	120 milliliters
1 cup	240 milliliters
1 pint (2 cups)	480 milliliters
1 quart (4 cups, 32 ounces)	960 milliliters
1 gallon (4 quarts)	3.84 liters
1 ounce (by weight)	28 grams
1 pound	454 grams
2.2 pounds	1 kilogram

1 medium lemon = 3 tablespoons juice

1 medium lime = 2 tablespoons juice

1 medium orange = ⅓ cup juice

OVEN TEMPERATURES

FAHRENHEIT	CELSIUS	GAS
250	120	½
275	140	1
300	150	2
325	160	3
350	180	4
375	190	5
400	200	6
425	220	7
450	230	8
475	240	9
500	260	10

LENGTH

U.S.	METRIC
⅛ inch	3 millimeters
¼ inch	6 millimeters
½ inch	12 millimeters
1 inch	2.5 centimeters